Piano • Vocal • Guitar

TOP CHRISTIAN HITS of 2011-2012

ISBN 978-1-4584-2069-5

HAL•LEONARD®
CORPORATION

7777 W. BLUEMOUND RD. P.O. BOX 13819 MILWAUKEE, WI 53213

For all works contained herein:
Unauthorized copying, arranging, adapting, recording, Internet posting, public performance,
or other distribution of the printed music in this publication is an infringement of copyright.
Infringers are liable under the law.

Visit Hal Leonard Online at
www.halleonard.com

BLESSINGS

Words and Music by
LAURA MIXON STORY

*Recorded a half step higher.

© 2011 New Spring Publishing (ASCAP) and Laura Stories (ASCAP)
All Rights Administered by New Spring Publishing
All Rights Reserved   Used by Permission

CHILDREN OF GOD

Words by MAC POWELL
Music by MAC POWELL, TAI ANDERSON,
DAVID CARR and MARK LEE

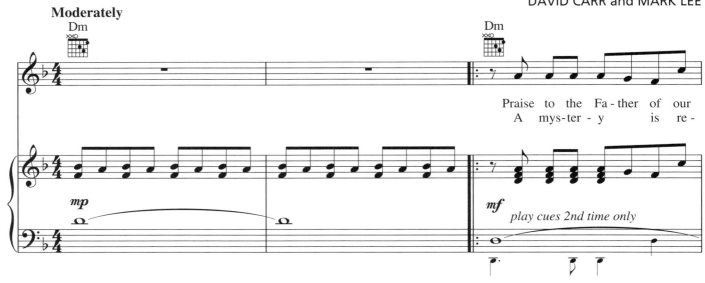

Praise to the Fa-ther of our
A mys-ter-y is re-

Lord Je-sus Christ, ___ our God and our King, ___ to Him we will sing. ___
vealed to the u-ni-verse. The Fa-ther a-bove ___ has prov-en His love. ___

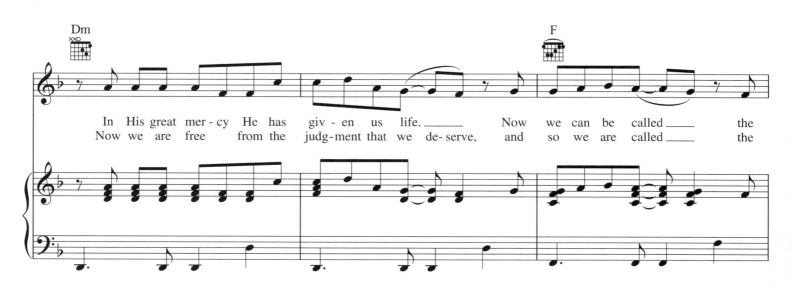

In His great mer-cy He has giv-en us life. ___ Now we can be called ___ the
Now we are free from the judg-ment that we de-serve, and so we are called ___ the

© 2010 SONGS FROM THE QUARRY (ASCAP)
Admin. at EMICMGPUBLISHING.COM
All Rights Reserved   Used by Permission

GOD'S NOT DEAD
(Like a Lion)

Words and Music by
DANIEL BASHTA

* *Recorded a half step lower.*

© 2010 WORSHIPTOGETHER.COM SONGS (ASCAP), sixsteps Music (ASCAP) and GO FORTH SOUNDS (ASCAP)
Admin. at EMICMGPUBLISHING.COM
All Rights Reserved   Used by Permission

COURAGEOUS

Words and Music by MARK HALL
and MATTHEW WEST

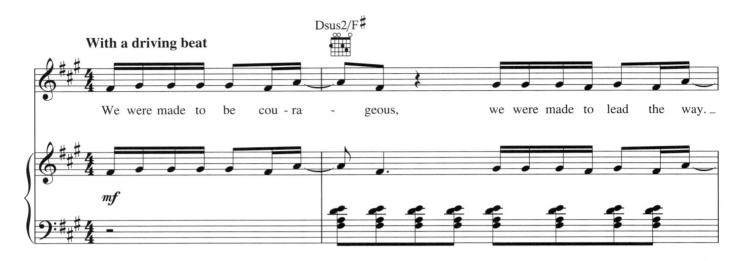

We were made to be cou-ra-geous, we were made to lead the way.

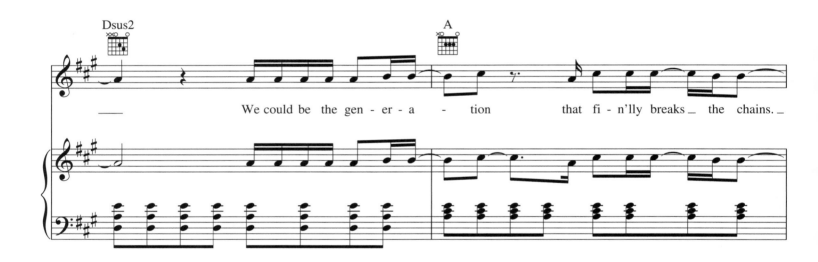

We could be the gen-er-a-tion that fi-n'lly breaks the chains.

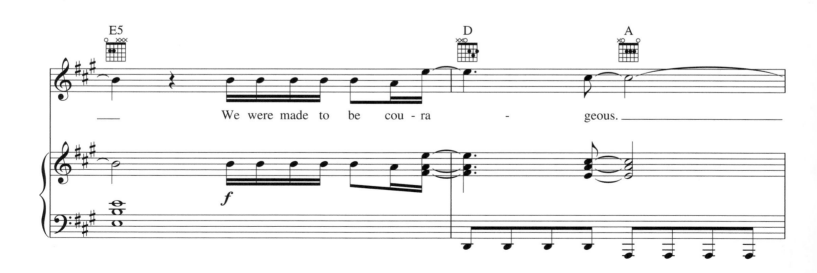

We were made to be cou-ra-geous.

Copyright © 2011 Sony/ATV Music Publishing LLC, My Refuge Music, Songs Of Southside Independent Music Publishing LLC, External Combustion Music and Songs For Delaney
All Rights on behalf of Sony/ATV Music Publishing LLC Administered by Sony/ATV Music Publishing LLC, 8 Music Square West, Nashville, TN 37203
All Rights on behalf of My Refuge Music Administered at EMICMGPublishing.com
All Rights on behalf of Songs Of Southside Independent Music Publishing LLC, External Combustion Music and Songs For Delaney Administered by WB Music Corp.
International Copyright Secured   All Rights Reserved

DO EVERYTHING

Words and Music by
STEVEN CURTIS CHAPMAN

* *Recorded a half step lower.*

Copyright © 2011 Primary Wave Brian (Chapman Sp Acct) and One Blue Petal Music
All Rights Administered by Wixen Music Publishing, Inc.
All Rights Reserved   Used by Permission

GLORIOUS DAY
(Living He Loved Me)

Words and Music by MARK HALL
and MICHAEL BLEAKER

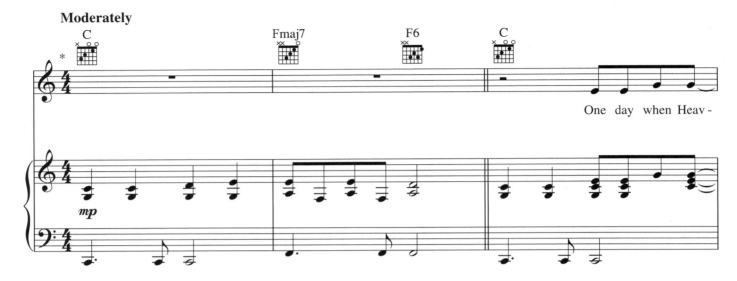

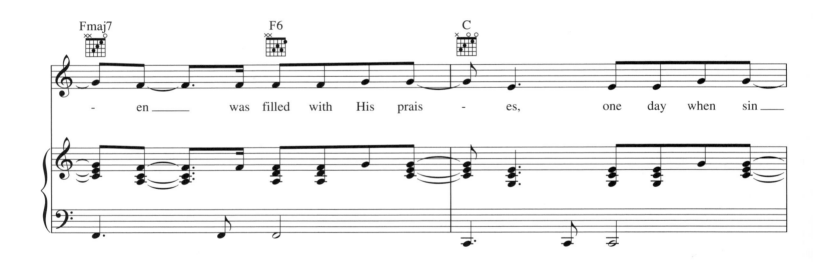

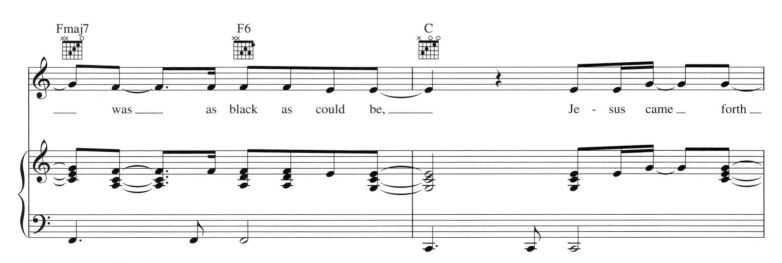

Recorded a half step lower.

© 2009 MY REFUGE MUSIC (BMI), SONY/ATV MUSIC PUBLISHING LLC (BMI) and WORD MUSIC, LLC (ASCAP)
MY REFUGE MUSIC Admin. at EMICMGPUBLISHING.COM
SONY/ATV MUSIC PUBLISHING LLC Admin. by SONY/ATV MUSIC PUBLISHING LLC, 8 Music Square West, Nashville, TN 37203
All Rights Reserved   Used by Permission

HOLD ME

Words and Music by CHRIS STEVENS,
TOBY McKEEHAN and JAMIE GRACE HARPER

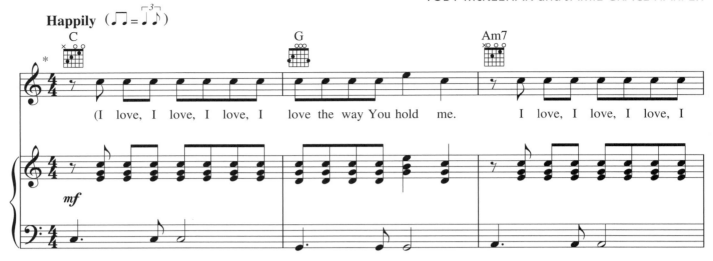

(I love, I love, I love, I love the way You hold me. I love, I love, I love, I

love the way You hold me.) love the way You, the way You...) I've had a long day; I just

wan- na re- lax. Don't have time ___ for my friends, _ no time ___ to chit - chat. Prob-

Recorded a half step lower.

© 2011 ACHTOBER SONGS (BMI), REGISFUNK MUSIC (BMI), UNIVERSAL MUSIC - BRENTWOOD BENSON TUNES (SESAC),
SONGS OF THIRD BASE (SESAC) and GRAPE JAM MUSIC (SESAC)
ACHTOBER SONGS and REGISFUNK MUSIC Admin. at EMICMGPUBLISHING.COM
SONGS OF THIRD BASE and GRAPE JAM MUSIC Admin. by UNIVERSAL MUSIC - BRENTWOOD BENSON TUNES
All Rights Reserved   Used by Permission

I LIFT MY HANDS

Words and Music by CHRIS TOMLIN,
LOUIE GIGLIO and MATT MAHER

* Recorded a half step lower.

© 2010 WORSHIPTOGETHER.COM SONGS (ASCAP), sixsteps Music (ASCAP), VAMOS PUBLISHING (ASCAP), VALLEY OF SONGS MUSIC (BMI) and THANKYOU MUSIC (PRS)
WORSHIPTOGETHER.COM SONGS, sixsteps Music, VAMOS PUBLISHING and VALLEY OF SONGS MUSIC Admin. at EMICMGPUBLISHING.COM
THANKYOU MUSIC Admin. Worldwide at EMICMGPUBLISHING.COM excluding Europe which is Admin. by Kingswaysongs
All Rights Reserved   Used by Permission

LIFT ME UP

Words and Music by MATT FUQUA,
JOSHUA HAVENS and DAN OSTEBO

Copyright © 2010 Demo Love Publishing, Smells Like Music, Screaming Mimes Music and Miracle In My Hand Music
All Rights Administered by Fair Trade Music Publishing
All Rights Reserved   Used by Permission

68

LISTEN TO THE SOUND

Words and Music by JASON ROY
and ROB HAWKINS

Copyright © 2011 Sony/ATV Music Publishing LLC, Havery Publishing and Pneumatic Man
All Rights on behalf of Sony/ATV Music Publishing LLC and Havery Publishing Administered by Sony/ATV Music Publishing LLC, 8 Music Square West, Nashville, TN 37203
International Copyright Secured   All Rights Reserved

THE LIGHT IN ME

Words and Music by BRANDON HEATH
and DANIEL MUCKALA

Moderate Rock beat

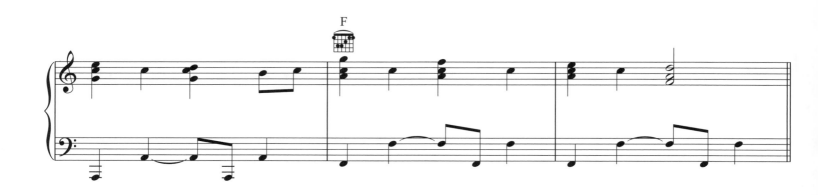

My life be-fore___ You,_____

Copyright © 2010 Sony/ATV Music Publishing LLC, Big Skwawka Music and Wintergone Music
All Rights on behalf of Sony/ATV Music Publishing LLC and Big Skwawka Music Administered by Sony/ATV Music Publishing LLC, 8 Music Square West, Nashville, TN 37203
All Rights on behalf of Wintergone Music Administered by Kobalt Music Publishing America, Inc.
International Copyright Secured   All Rights Reserved

MOVE

Words and Music by JAMES BRYSON,
NATHAN COCHRAN, BARRY GRAUL,
BART MILLARD, DANIEL MUCKALA,
MICHAEL SCHEUCHZER and ROBIN SHAFFER

With energy

I'm not a-bout to give __ up, be-cause I heard You say, __

__ there's gon-na be bright - er days, __ there's gon-na be bright - er days. __

I won't stop; I'll keep my head __ up. No, I'm not here to stay. __

Copyright © 2010 Simpleville Music, Wet As A Fish Music and Wintergone Music
All Rights for Simpleville Music and Wet As A Fish Music Administered by Simpleville Music, Inc.
All Rights for Wintergone Music Administered by Kobalt Music Publishing America, Inc.
International Copyright Secured   All Rights Reserved

THE REDEEMER

Words and Music by MATT HAMMITT,
CHRIS ROHMAN, MARK GRAALMAN,
DAN GARTLEY, PETER PREVOST
and CHRIS STEVENS

© 2009 BIRDWING MUSIC (ASCAP), REGISFUNK MUSIC (BMI), OLDE IRISH PUBLISHING (BMI), TOLEDO TOMORROW MUSIC (ASCAP), 1012 ROSEDALE MUSIC (ASCAP),
EVEN-THO MUSIC (ASCAP), LOOK AT MY BEARD (ASCAP), STONEBROOK MUSIC COMPANY (SESAC) and RIVER OAKS MUSIC COMPANY (BMI)
Admin. at EMICMGPUBLISHING.COM
All Rights Reserved   Used by Permission

I don't have ev - er - y an -

- swer in life, ___ but I'm trust - ing You ___ one day ___

SMS
(Shine)

Words and Music by DAVID CROWDER
and JACK PARKER

Moderately slow

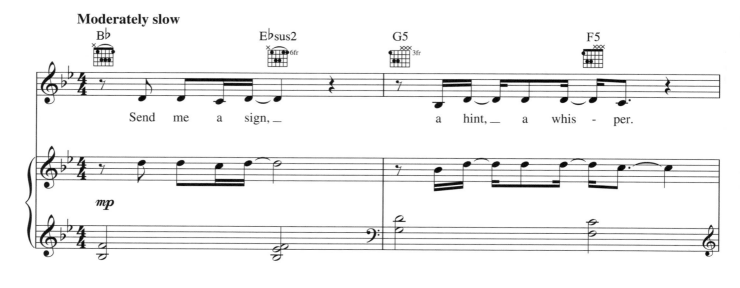

Send me a sign, ___ a hint, ___ a whis - per.

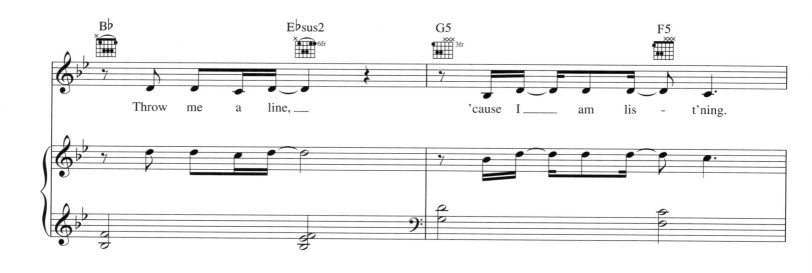

Throw me a line, ___ 'cause I ___ am lis - t'ning.

Come break the quiet, ___ breathe Your a - wak - en - ing. ___

© 2009 WORSHIPTOGETHER.COM SONGS (ASCAP), sixsteps Music (ASCAP) and INOT MUSIC (ASCAP)
Admin. at EMICMGPUBLISHING.COM
All Rights Reserved   Used by Permission

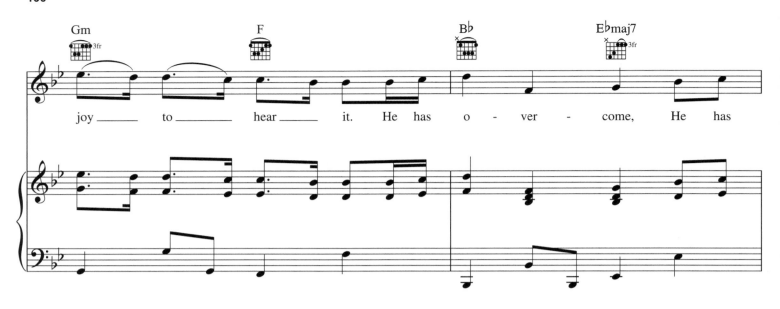

joy _____ to _____ hear _____ it. He has o - ver - come, He has

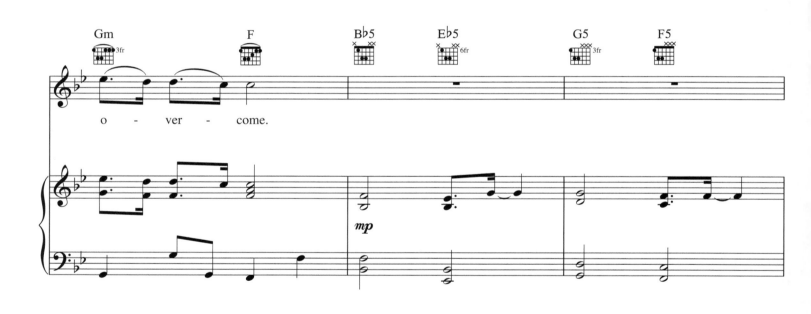

o - ver - come.

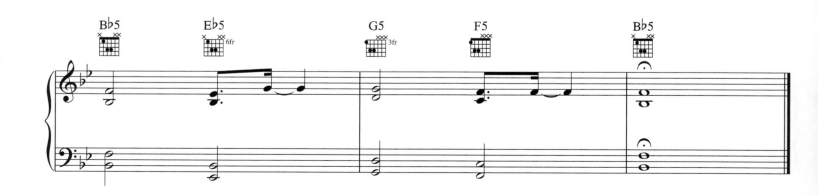

TRUST IN JESUS

Words by MAC POWELL
Music by MAC POWELL, TAI ANDERSON,
DAVID CARR and MARK LEE

Moderate Rock beat

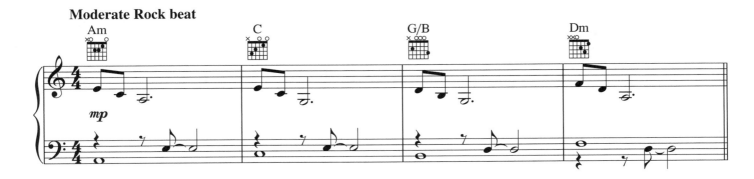

One of these days we all will stand in judg - ment for ev - 'ry sin -

- gle word that we have spo - ken.

© 2010 SONGS FROM THE QUARRY (ASCAP)
Admin. at EMICMGPUBLISHING.COM
All Rights Reserved   Used by Permission

STRONG ENOUGH TO SAVE

Words and Music by MIKE DONEHEY,
JASON INGRAM and PHILLIP LaRUE

Copyright © 2009, 2010 Sony/ATV Music Publishing LLC, Formerly Music, Deeper Still Music Publishing and My Maxx Songs
All Rights on behalf of Sony/ATV Music Publishing LLC and Formerly Music Administered by Sony/ATV Music Publishing LLC, 8 Music Square West, Nashville, TN 37203
All Rights on behalf of Deeper Still Music Publishing and My Maxx Songs Administered by Songs Of Razor & Tie d/b/a Razor & Tie Music Publishing, LLC
International Copyright Secured   All Rights Reserved

STRONGER

Words and Music by BEN GLOVER,
CHRIS STEVENS and DAVID GARCIA

Pop R&B feel

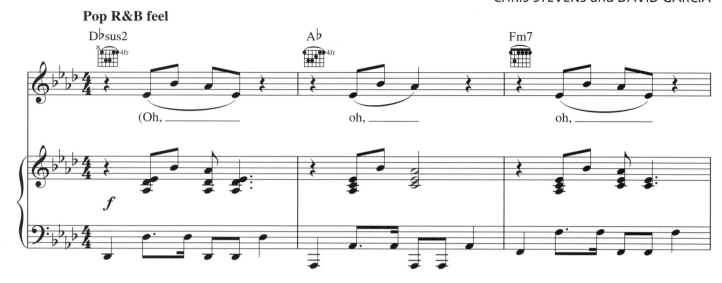

(Oh, _____ oh, _____ oh, _____

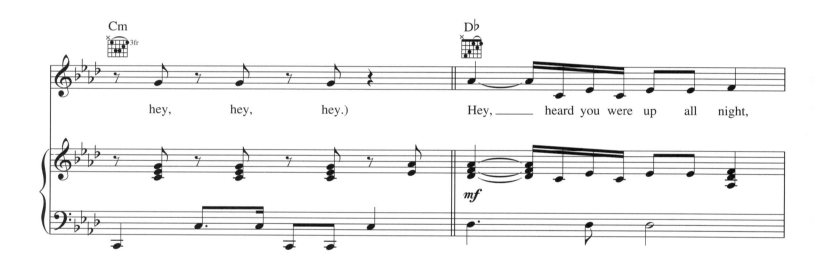

hey, hey, hey.) Hey, _____ heard you were up all night,

think-ing 'bout how your world ain't right, and you won-der if things _ will nev-er get

© 2011 REGISFUNK MUSIC (BMI), 9T ONE SONGS (ASCAP), ARIOSE MUSIC (ASCAP), UNIVERSAL MUSIC - BRENTWOOD BENSON PUBLISHING (ASCAP) and D SOUL MUSIC (ASCAP)
REGISFUNK MUSIC, 9T ONE SONGS and ARIOSE MUSIC Admin. at EMICMGPUBLISHING.COM
D SOUL MUSIC Admin. Worldwide by UNIVERSAL MUSIC - BRENTWOOD BENSON PUBLISHING
All Rights Reserved Used by Permission

TURN AROUND

Words and Music by MATT MAHER,
MICHAEL BOGGS and TREVOR MORGAN

Young man __ on the side of the road, __ lost __ __ and beat __ up with no - where to go. __ Smells __ like a hang - o - ver from __

© 2010 THANKYOU MUSIC (PRS), UPSURGE MUSIC L.L.C. (ASCAP), VALLEY OF SONGS MUSIC (BMI) and TREVOR MORGAN MUSIC (ASCAP)
THANKYOU MUSIC Admin. Worldwide at EMICMGPUBLISHING.COM excluding Europe which is Admin. by Kingswaysongs
UPSURGE MUSIC L.L.C. and VALLEY OF SONGS MUSIC Admin. at EMICMGPUBLISHING.COM
All Rights Reserved   Used by Permission

THE WAY

Words and Music by JEREMY CAMP,
BRAD PEENS, ROB WILLIAMS
and GRANT DRYDEN

© 2010 THIRSTY MOON RIVER PUBLISHING (ASCAP), STOLEN PRIDE MUSIC (ASCAP) and BLUKE MUSIC PUBLISHING (ASCAP)
Admin. at EMICMGPUBLISHING.COM
All Rights Reserved   Used by Permission

YOUR GREAT NAME

Words and Music by MICHAEL NEALE
and KRISSY NORDHOFF

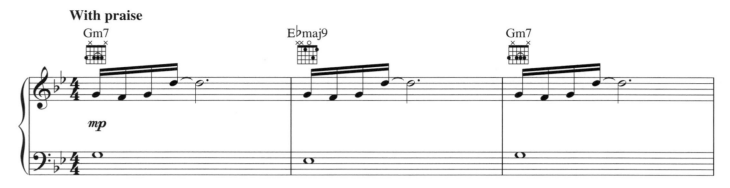

Lost are _____ saved, find their _____ way at the sound _____

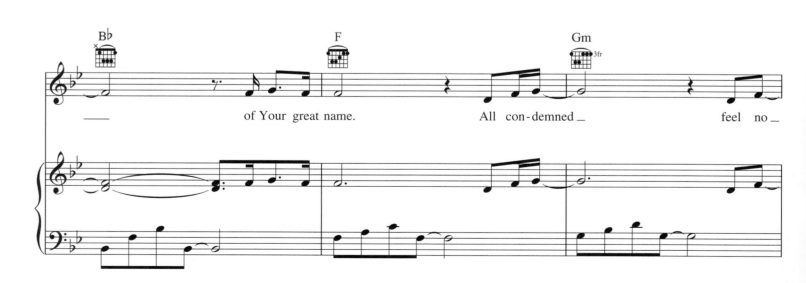

_____ of Your great name. All con-demned _____ feel no _____

© 2008 INTEGRITY'S PRAISE! MUSIC (BMI) and TWONORDS MUSIC (ASCAP)
INTEGRITY'S PRAISE! MUSIC Admin. at EMICMGPUBLISHING.COM
TWONORDS MUSIC Admin. Worldwide by MUSIC SERVICES, INC., www.musicservices.org
All Rights Reserved   Used by Permission

YOU ARE MORE

Words and Music by JASON INGRAM
and MIKE DONEHEY

Moderately slow Rock, in 2

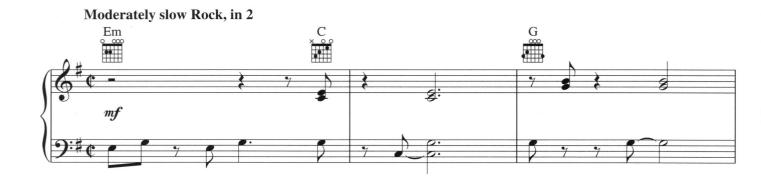

There's a girl in ___ the cor - ner

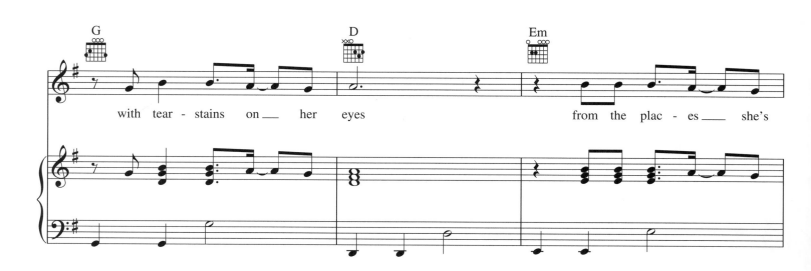

with tear - stains on ___ her eyes   from the plac - es ___ she's

Copyright © 2010 Sony/ATV Music Publishing LLC, Windsor Hill Music and Formerly Music
All Rights Administered by Sony/ATV Music Publishing LLC, 8 Music Square West, Nashville, TN 37203
International Copyright Secured   All Rights Reserved